THE SUPERPOWER OF THE GIRL CHILD

- TRANSCENDING GENDER BIAS AND OVERCOMING OBSTACLES

CATHELINE MAHUTO

DEDICATION

First, I would like to thank God for allowing me to live, learn, love and share the gift of life.

I would like to dedicate this book to my children Samson, Kudakwashe, Barbara and Cecilia and to my wonderful grandchildren Amanda, Kundai, Mikaela, Munaye, Ethan, Shariah, Mutsawashe, Seth, Zoe, Asher , Savannah and Riley and great grandchildren Juju, Tegan, Teddy. I would like to extend my thank you to my parents Levy and Elizabeth Mauto and all my siblings. Thanks to all my siblings and family and all my friends and thanks to HerStory for making this possible for me.

CONTENTS

FOREWORD

When Catheline first informed me she was writing this book, it encouraged me. Mainly because it's a story that needs to be shared with the entire world, a true story of finding the sunshine after the rain, finding the light at the end of the tunnel, taking the first step even though one can't see the entire staircase.

I know firsthand how hard it was to relive these stories in order to articulate them in a way that you, the reader, can benefit from them, and I truly hope that you will find inspiration between the pages of this book.

No matter if you are a man or woman, we were all born from a woman and understanding this story may help you understand the women in your life and what they go through and how you can better serve them.

If you are a woman, then I know for sure that you will receive nuggets you can use to grow in your relationships and in your own personal and professional life.

One story that moved me the most was the tenacity of Catheline to overcome her own fears in order to educate herself and her family. The fight she put up to maintain her own sanity and that of her children even while she went through untold suffering and that not of her choosing. And last, the key thing I love about this book is that it's not just a reading book but a book bent on helping people to find solutions rather than to just sharing stories.

Cee Jay Besa

Author, Speaker and Trainer

PREFACE

I would like to thank you for purchasing this book. I am truly grateful that you have invested in yourself by picking this book. A brief history. When I wrote this book, it didn't start out as a book; it started out as a compilation of my family history. My children had asked me about their family tree.

So I began compiling names and creating a family tree and as I explained the family tree I kept getting questions about how these individuals were involved in my life and what the stories were behind certain people whom they did not know, including their fathers. While I normally share these stories with people that I counsel or podiums where I speak, I realised that my family hardly knew some of these stories, and as I shared, I recognized right away how some puzzles in their lives were being resolved.

So, with this information I took a broader approach and instead of just writing a story of my life, I put together the stories that my family and my audiences are always curious about and want to know how I made it back then. I then compiled these into what became the book entitled The Super Power Of The Girl Child.

In the pages of this book I shared my highest highs and my lowest lows but only with a desire to help you the reader to make faith, make sense, find hope and tools to use in order to transcend the gender biases that you and your children may face in life.

CATHELINE MAHUTO

1 GIRL CHILD CHRONICLES

My faith did not remove the pain, but my faith got me through the pain. - Catheline Mahuto

Trusting God on my journey in life didn't diminish my hope but enabled me to endure it, and now I can share my story.

My name is Catheline Mahuto I am sixty-eight years old. I live in the United Kingdom on the outskirts of London. I migrated from Zimbabwe to the United Kingdom in 2003.

I am a Zimbabwean born in Southern Rhodesia during colonial rule, in a small town called Bindura.

Southern Rhodesia is now Zimbabwe named after gaining its independence from Britain in 1980.

I prefer to be called Katie; the reason is my parents never called me by my full name so everyone in my family or friends know me as Katie. Although I have a traditional Shona name my parents called me by as well, that name is not on my birth certificate.

Colonial rulers, which were mostly Caucasian and also foreign, recorded most of our birth details. They worked at the registry offices and they often misspelled native names because of language barriers and sometimes even missed the very crucial details that were supposed to be added to our birth certificates.

As a result, so many families found themselves with the same last name with various spellings yet born of the same parents.

I am the first child in a family of nine, six girls and three boys. My father was born to a Malawian father and his mother was a Zimbabwean.

Meanwhile, on the maternal side they are also mixed-race grandparents. My grandfather came from the north through neighbouring Botswana and settled in Zimbabwe. What a beautiful brand of history. I am blessed with this mix because it has made me beautiful and to interact with a few languages which I can speak. I didn't fully master their dialects, so I am not very fluent because they didn't live long enough to teach me much more and mostly all I knew I had learned from them. Like where exactly they came from, their culture and languages as well. So, I miss that bit of my history and that heritage is vague.

I am a single mother of four grownup children, two boys and two girls, now I am a grandmother of twelve and great- grandmother to three boys.

In this book, I will speak about how I went through harrowing experiences in my marriages several times and how they all came to zero, ending in divorces. My parents, as with other cultures, believed in arranged marriages to safeguard the future of their girl child.

So, my parents did the same thing after my basic primary education. My parents thought it was ideal for me to get married so they could save the limited resources for their boys to go further with their education. In those times girls were always being portrayed as second class in many cultures right across the globe it would appear.

As a girl they always reminded you that your place is the kitchen and childbearing. Be submissive. Remain under your husband or your brothers. They came first before you.

I had my own dreams though, as I was growing up, each time I visited the hospital I had a dream that one day I was going to become a nurse and wear that white uniform with those medals, a green or red belt and that white headscarf. I spent much of my time daydreaming and imagining that I would get there one day. Unfortunately, I did not fulfill that dream and I looked at it as a failed dream in those days.

The reason I failed to attain that dream was at thirteen years old my parents told me I was to be married. That announcement shocked me. Imagine watching your classmates proceeding to secondary school and onto higher education and carrying the same hope! It was my desire as well, but this was the end of my formal education journey. My pending marriage closed that door.

I pleaded with my parents, but the deal was to get married first, then maybe the husband was going to agree to send me back to school, but to no avail.

Imagine getting married to a man or woman you never proposed or chose? Imagine you marry a person whom you do not know who they are but having a conversation of love when you meet for the first time?

What about getting intimate with a stranger they have introduced you to as your husband/wife what will be your feelings towards this stranger? Was I not allowed to fall in love first? I remember asking myself over and over with no answers.

After much crying, pleading, and protesting, I agreed to this arrangement. The man paid the dowry, and I was married off. My father sent me to a homecraft college, which was the best he could do in those circumstances. This was a school for adult learners and most of them married women. It taught us practical skills on how to carry out your role as a woman or wife in your home.

There I spent two years learning how to prepare food, knitting, garment making, crotchet and gardening. As someone whose desire was to be a nurse, I was miserable for two years. How does a thirteen-year-old relate to full grown women?

I could not understand why my parents sent me there, but in my later years, this training became essential to my life and that of my children. I made a decision that if I was going to be at the college, then I was also going to learn some of these life skills, and these would later serve me in my life to this day. When I completed this course, I was still underage, but I was now married, so I had to proceed to my arranged marriage. If I could compare it to anything, it would seem to resemble a halfway house into marriage.

The man who married me refused to accept me. He was educated and working at a prestigious institution and did not see reason to proceed with this marriage; he felt I was beneath him. I had almost come to terms with being forced into marriage, and now I was going through a crash course on being rejected. Think of any 15-year-old that you know. Are they yet equipped to handle rejection?

With tears in his eyes, he said you are too young to be my wife; you are still underage; you are better off going back to school but this was after losing two years after my primary education?

Let's work with this information

1. What is your expectation for your life as a girlchild?
2. If you are a parent what is your outlook for your girlchildren
3. How well are you preparing your children for your own cultural challenges and beliefs?
4. How do you handle rejection, do you teach your children how to handle rejection?
5. Your girl child will face a lot of gender bias, how well are you preparing them for such a future?
6. Have you lost time due to other people's decisions on your life, how can you make up for the time now?
7. What are you doing to prepare them for a successful marriage?

THE SUPER POWER OF THE GIRL CHILD

2 NEW BEGINNINGS

They sent me home packing the following day to my parents, but this was an immense blow on my parents, who had to return the dowry. By that time, I am certain they had already spent the dowry money on other things and could not refund that money right away. They were expecting us to go through with this arrangement, and all came to a halt.

They did not understand it, so they found yet another man for me, and they arranged another marriage within a short time. I went through three arranged marriages and nothing worked. Maybe I was now becoming annoyed by it all, so I was no longer fully engaging, but felt powerless to say no. As a girl child you are to be married, period and that was the statement that I kept hearing, so it became a belief at that tender age.

I was dealing with rejection on both sides, my parents and the two failed marriages.

Who else could say they had two failed marriages by 17 years of age? At this stage the husband who took me in was older, almost my father's age. He was abusive towards me and did not care that I was still an underage child, unlike the other two. Soon, I fell pregnant at seventeen and gave birth to my first child just before my eighteenth birthday, a son. We named him Samson.

My husband did not allow me to see my friends, especially those from my primary school who had proceeded further with education. I could not could not talk back to him and each time I did I received a severe beating with feasts and punches. I was a wife and treated like a daughter at the same time yet I was the age of what would have been a daughter to him. Meanwhile, there was no turning back or retreat to my parents because there was a lot of resistance after they had returned a dowry earlier on, so it was game on. There was no turning back until the day my then husband nearly killed me with severe physical beatings.

My father said it was enough, and he unilaterally took me back home. I had a child, my son who was almost seven months. I could not carry my baby because of the injuries. Luckily, I survived this abuse hence I am sharing this story today too and hope that it helps someone.

I went through a bitter divorce with this man, and it left me with my son. I thought I had understood the abuse and was now wise enough to avoid such but unfortunately; I had not learned my lesson well. In addition, the fact remained that my only option was to get married again as I was still under my parents' roof, except this time I was not alone, I now had a son.

In my language they have demeaning terms for a single woman with a child. The term is "Mvana". Your parents and those around you may even stop calling you by name and refer to you as Mvana.

I moved to live with Uncle William, who was my father's younger brother. I lived there briefly so that I could attend Speciss College to get a secretarial qualification. He had high hopes for me to send me abroad for the sake of education, but my parents thwarted this move.

I was feeling healed now from that last divorce and I decided perhaps it was time to meet the man of my dreams. Indeed, I met a man who I believed was closer to my age, who was my choice and who was going to be a better husband. He was young at my age and what was not to love about that, so I fell head over heels in love with him. My new husband knew I had a son from the previous marriage. He even supported the idea of my child before we got married and promised to take me and my child as well.

I was happy with this arrangement and married my then Romeo. Our union was quick, and we could not wait to be wed in matrimony. One day, my gentleman of quick wit and chivalry showed up at my father's house wearing a nice grey suit and invited me to go out with him. We went to a local high fashion store called Thurlow's and there he had me select the most beautiful dress. It was a bright yellow dress, the kind that celebrities like Diana Ross and Aretha Franklin would wear in those days.

We went to the court and became man and wife, and he whisked me off my feet. This was how I imagined it would be. You fall in love and marry the one you love and choose.

Not long after, we moved into our home in the city, in a suburb called Mabvuku. I fell pregnant and gave birth to a baby girl, whom I named Barbara. She was a bubbly baby who cried through the night most days and was attached to her mother at the hip such that it was difficult to leave her anywhere with anyone else. I had left my son with my parents for the time being while we settled. I was now preparing for my son to join us after giving birth, but my husband Joe did not want my son to come and join us.

My parents sent my son with my brother Stoney to visit us and to see my newborn baby. My husband did not want to see my son, and he sent him away crying in the morning having been told the same. This situation devastated me. I could not understand what had changed. How do you prepare for a situation where you have a husband who refuses to take in your son? This situation conflicted me deeply.

It was while Stoney visited that day that he found out they were recruiting for the army and he became interested and signed up. He dropped my son off with our parents and departed and I would not see him again for years as the country was also at war.

By the time my newborn daughter turned one, my husband had a mistress who was now almost six months pregnant. He did not want me to know, but the mistress made sure I knew because she showed up at my work in a front store at the time and provoked me. My husband was very business savvy and had an uncle who entrusted him with much of his business dealings, so he was always doing well financially. He had entrusted us to run a particular grocery store, and I was in front of the operation.

One day a woman whom I was not familiar with showed up and spoke with my husband. They carried on for a while until they went outside. I could tell by the body language that there was some misunderstanding between them. She returned into the store and started insulting me and I was trying to ignore at first, giving her the benefit of a doubt that perhaps she was just having a bad day. I felt this was a direct personal attack. Being young and naïve regrettably, I leaped over the store counter and confronted this woman. My intuition was telling me she had some skin in the game, she had something to lose or gain by this provocation.

That was the day my marriage ended in my heart; I did not look at my husband the same as before anymore. He became a guest in our marital home and though we had wed, instead of being the wife, I became his mistress. He only came home when he felt like passing by. I am sure he felt some way about the altercation as well. His mistress left in terrible pain because even though she had a mouth on her, she was not a fighter. I am the firstborn of 9, can you imagine how much fighting I had to do to gain respect from my younger brothers who felt tougher than me, I was tough because of that but I regretted the fight so much I never got into any other physical confrontations after this.

I was now being treated as an option, like being told if you want to leave feel free but vaguely where he would not spell this out. He came by and slept at home once in a while so; I fell pregnant again not because we fixed things between us, but that I had the hope that we could mend our marriage as before. I was learning, however, that sex does not fix broken trust.

Let us now get to work with this chapter.

1. Have you taken time to know the person you are with, don't be in a hurry to fall into a relationship?

2. Have you felt rejected and cheated on by a spouse? Are you taking time to analyze what has led to this issue?

3. How can you create a safe environment for you and your spouse to discuss pertinent matters that help you to know each other before becoming sexually active?

4. Analyze your own character when provoked, are there things you need to change when responding.

5. Do you take time to heal or hurry into the next relationship?

6. If you come into a relationship with your own child, do you choose to stay if your spouse decides not to accept your child?

7. Why or why not?

CATHELINE MAHUTO

3 THE AWAKENING

It was on 10 August when my husband came home and spent the night. In my sleep I dreamed I was trying to use the bathroom and I woke up with a strange pain. My waters had broken, and I was in labour.

My husband noticed that but instead of him supporting me through this period he simply got up, dressed and drove off, leaving me with no one to take me to the hospital and deliver. He simply drove off.

He had a car, few people around there had private cars as a means of transportation.

Meanwhile, the labour pain was now intense, and I called out to him. No one answered my call but our neighbour saw my husband leave that morning, so she came to my rescue noticing that I was in labour and needed urgent help. She summoned other fast thinking mothers in the area who got me an ambulance and in time I was in the maternity ward where I delivered a baby boy alone without Joe to witness the birth of our second baby.

I had no one to check on me or bring me food since this was a new hospital, so there was no provision for food. New mothers who had given birth shared their food with me for three days. When I got discharged, I came out with my baby and a bag of baby's nappies. I had to walk for two miles. It was not the easiest thing to do, as I was still in pain from the delivery. After delivery, it's one of those things were you ain't got to go home but you got to get up out of here.

After I had walked for a while, I stopped to adjust the baby, who I carried on my back in a towel wrapped around him. It appears luck found me that instant when I noticed that school was dismissed and the children were going home. They came to my rescue, and they carried my baby and the bag home. I was so grateful and thanked them for getting me home safe. This was to be my networking baby, a smiling and cheerful baby who would play with one thing in fascination for hours; he was very active going everywhere around the house. He would grow up to be very athletic and just a wonderful kid to most people who knew him. My mother named him Kudakwashe, meaning God's will.

It felt as if I had no husband; I felt as if I was all alone but I went through with it. At the time it appeared there was no light at the end of the tunnel, but I had not given up hope that one day he would come home and see the sense that this was his primary home. With great distress, I learned his mistress had a second child around that same time. Now I thought perhaps he was more committed to his mistress. I surely could not tell and didn't want to believe it, either.

But I had nowhere to go back to. Remember the difference this time is that I chose him. This man was my choice, not an arranged marriage so I had one obligation and that was to make this marriage work. I committed to that even as my heart was torn apart. Things carried on the same way. He would come home sometimes and spend a few hours, then leave in the middle of the night.

I kept reflecting on what I might do next while I sat outside in a daze most of that day. Eventually, I must have found my way into my house and fell on my bed and slept. When I woke up, it was the next morning. My husband packed all our bags and dumped us at my parents' home with no explanation. Meanwhile, I now had three children who needed support, and this move did not impress my parents. They were going to send me back the following day. Unfortunately, I fell sick with a rare disease and had to be hospitalized for three months.

My husband heard about this but never came forward to see about the children's welfare, neither did it appear to matter about my well-being. My son, a newborn of two months, was now being cared for by my mother, who by then had advanced in age. In the three months during my hospitalization, my husband only visited me once until I got discharged. By then my baby was almost six months old. He could not recognize me; he was now crawling; you can imagine he had not seen me for three months. At first, he would not come near me, but I guess maternal bond is strong. Eventually, here he was, coming in for hugs.

During the time I was sick, they say they fed me through a tube while I was in what appeared to be a coma. Rumour has it that while I was in hospital Uncle William, the youngest sibling to my father, had an encounter with my now estranged husband at a shopping centre called Machipisa. It was a good hangout place for men and they would socialize and drink alcohol there. He confronted my ex, saying your wife lies in a hospital and you have not had the heart to come and visit even once?

When the man professed innocence and pleaded that he was unaware, my uncle laid it on him with a flurry of punches and kicks. He was angry; he was having to drive every day for miles to come and bring the kids food and make sure I was well, meanwhile this guy Joe was hanging out at a bar, eating barbeque and sipping cold beer. They say it was a heated encounter and Joe did not return the punches. Out of respect and perhaps a little fear, instead he ran away on foot, leaving his car behind.

That would likely be when he came to the hospital, and a few days later I was discharged to go home. After I recovered and could travel, my parents sent me back without checking if my safety was guaranteed or if I was safe on my return to my matrimonial home. They did not appear concerned enough to follow through if all was going to be okay. No one cared to ask will he be accepting me and the children, seeing as he had partaken little during the months gone by, which to me was a telling sign of things to come.

We arrived home late, and everyone in the neighbourhood was fast asleep. All our furniture and belongings in the house were gone, not because they robbed us. My husband had officially moved in with his mistress into a new neighbourhood called Unit N. Our clothes were in a newspaper spread on the floor. My children and I slept in the cold that night with no blankets.

This is a very sensitive story for me, but I tell you this story for a reason. I know you may feel discouraged, broken-hearted, betrayed, hurt and everything else in between, similar or worse to what I shared in this story, but I am here to tell you this is not the end for you. I kept on saying to myself this is not the end for me.

You have a superpower deep within you. You must tap into and let that mind power to lead the way. I did not know my uncle would fight for me. As much as I don't condone violence, still it makes one feel good when there is at least one person in the world that will fight for you. I was in a state because I felt betrayed by some of my friends around us and is it any wonder I felt that way? But God always keeps at least one person fighting for you. Sometimes it's the most unlikely person and sometimes even a stranger.

Right now, as I write the pages of this book, I am fighting for you and I believe that out of this content, something I shared is helping you right now.

Let us now get to work with this chapter.

1. What about this story has resonated with you?

2. Why did that resonate with you?

3. What are the take aways for you from this story?

4. Who has betrayed you that needs to be let go?

5. Who has harmed you that you need to forgive?

6. Who has been there fighting for you that you have not yet acknowledged?

7. How can you outgrow the pains and the challenges, what or who can you look into their eyes for courage and hope?

8. Can you see hope for your future and does this chapter inspire you to see there is more ahead of you?

CATHELINE MAHUTO

4 BACK LIKE I NEVER LEFT

As I contemplated what I might do next, there didn't appear to be too many options, I was forced to remember that I chose to disobey my parents when I didn't accept the arranged marriages and this man was my choice so the option was "continue with your journey Missy".

I was back in my matrimonial home like I had never left so it was time to dance to the music, so far, I was not liking the tune. My husband did not turn up home as usual, instead his father arrived the following day to help me with the children relocate to his rural homestead which I did as long as I still had a place to stay with my children all was going to be well. We got on a bus and travelled to the village of Seke.

I kept telling myself "One day it was going to be well and my marriage was going to work". So, with this in my mind and looking at my two children meanwhile my older son was now in his father's custody due to these ups and downs where he couldn't be with me nor could he be with my parents. I always reminded myself that one day I was going to have my children under one roof one day.

After a few days my husband came to see how I was settling at his rural home. I had never stayed in a rural setting. My parents stayed in town. I came from the middle class where my parents were not rich, but they were working class, so this had to be my first experience in this setting. I had no issues with it for the sake of my children. I fitted in slowly. I did well because I was taught these things early at the homecraft mission college, so nothing was amiss. Also, my mother's training as a girl child came in handy at this time.

My husband did not say anything, nor did he show any signs that I must not be there. Maybe he was convicted on the idea of dumping me at my parents' home without explaining the reason of divorce or separation through the court as prescribed by the law. It took a very high level of restraint on my end to not provoke a conversation or retaliate for the removal of our belongings. I was becoming more self-aware, no one could upset me if I didn't choose to be upset.

So, this time I was going to go with the flow, so I now took on the role of his mistress. And I had no obligation but to wait for him to come home when he wanted or when he saw fit. I still respected him as my husband remember as a wife you have to be submissive right, so life continued in that manner. Many times, we ran short of food and my mother-in-law provided food for us. In her conviction she used to say this is the behavior of many men. They do this to their wives but at the end the men get tired and they settle, how sad.

This situation went on with my husband dashing in and out when he saw fit. One morning his father fell sick and passed on while I was taking care of him. My mother in-law had travelled to visit her siblings. I found myself coordinating this program where I had many people coming from all over the country for this funeral. After a while, my husband came to make some arrangements for his father's burial. I suppose he did not tell his mistress about this, but she somehow found out and she also came on her own to pay her last respects.

When she arrived, she noticed that I was there and heavily pregnant she confronted my husband and asked him why I was there and pregnant. Who was the father of that baby? He had told her I was no longer with him, that he was waiting for a divorce at the court. Of course, this was not true he was being a coward and not standing by his actions. His uncle intervened and sent her away to avoid the embarrassment at a funeral.

This kind of commotion at a funeral is unacceptable particularly if the reason you came was to show your respects of the late. Soon after the funeral, my husband left without a word and since it had become the norm it didn't make any difference to me. But after this embarrassment and confrontation it was time for him to make a move. What would be his move, I wondered?

One thing was clear, he wanted to prove to his mistress that he had truly moved on. However, I'm sure she was not convinced since she had seen me pregnant at the funeral, so my assumption is she needed things cemented. He would need to find a way to prove that I was no longer his wife. I was almost eight months pregnant and anyway I didn't have the heart to confront him or the poor girl, she was also caught up in this mess now and I rather felt compassion for her.

I was watching my temper and not allowing things to bother me as I was far along in my pregnancy. I was also partly accepting that she was in our lives and to add to that, I was serious impediment to their relationship because I was being supported by his mother in their home. My mother in-law never wavered, she stood by her word I was going to stay there come rain come sunshine.

I know vividly the taste of salty tears effortless running down your face, and I know what depression is, I had all in that season. I was hurting, embarrassed, confused but it was not time for me to leave yet, I was about the business of having this baby and she came just a couple of months after the funeral of his father

Then came the day that I would never forget, this was the day he was going to wed with his mistress, and by my intuition I could just sense it in the air.

You know when people are trying hard not to say anything, but you can just feel that there is something people are not telling you?

It seemed like any ordinary Saturday and I was sweeping up the dusty yard of our village home, I noticed that many key family members who would normally be cleaning up or getting ready for the weekend activities were not around. Where on earth is everyone today, I wondered. Anyway, I carried on with my household chores and was thinking how strange the last few weeks had been.

My husband would come and visit, and he would be brief in his visits, he would not leave any money for food or talk to the children. He would walk in, make small talk, sit a few minutes then, walk right out and drive away into the neighborhood. Then much later he would either swing by or speed past the house on his way to his mistress house where he now lived. I expected that he would show up that Saturday as usual but, he never did.

I noticed that in the days gone past he was now being very harsh and belligerent with me and my guess was that he thought the rough treatment would push me to just leave. He wasn't aware what I was dealing with, there was nowhere for me to go. Staying with his mother was my only remaining option at this point. While I was reflecting on these thoughts sitting outside, I saw a young boy who was our nephew and he was happy and excited to announce that he was coming from the wedding and wanted to know why I didn't attend.

Whose wedding did you come from I inquired curiously, he said Uncle Joe's wedding meaning my husband. Oh, you better believe I was livid, and I went from zero to hundred and back to zero in just one second. You mean to tell me the entire neighbourhood went to this wedding at our local church and no one told me about it? Have you ever felt that people hid a secret from you and you alone? That felt like betrayal of the highest order. Our young nephew carried on with his merry self, oblivious to the broken heart his joyful news had caused.

Slowly the neighbours started trickling in, which was a sign that the festivities were over. I didn't try to go up and confront anyone as I was made weak by the news and the deceit. I just sat there against the wall of the house, staring blankly at the road. I wasn't thinking anything I was blank, I wasn't feeling anything, I was numb, I just sat there. I am sure many people came and passed with some sort of greetings, but I don't remember responding to anyone. It was like a bad dream but where you have no power to wake up and snap out of it. The entire day must have come and went while I sat there maybe half-awake half in a daze.

Later that year I welcomed my last-born baby girl and named her Cecilia after my ex-husband's mother. My husband didn't come to see our baby and I guess, previously I was waiting to be told that it was over, but now I knew it was over. I put that baby on my back and did the usual walk back home. She was a big beautiful baby with a smile and joyful laughter that would light up my heart each time she chuckled as she still does today.

She was my bubble of joy she was my hope for the future and as I looked into those eyes, I was inspired to dream bigger, go further and farther.

My husband returned drunk a few days later with

some level of anger and chose to physically beat me up. This time I had a baby in the house and she somehow fell and rolled beneath the couch so that she was not injured thank God. Someone in the family intervened since we were now in a village setting where everyone's business is your business too.

I stayed with his mom that night while the family tried to solve our issues, but it was the day I told myself that was the final straw, I couldn't go further, I had enough, and he had crossed the line. I made a decision; it was my time to leave. Never would I allow anyone to lay their hands on me again , not me, no way, no sir.

I was not going to stay in this abusive marriage. I was

now looking ahead and here was my first action step. I was going to take responsibility for my own actions, I was going to get all my children including my first child and look after them by myself no matter what. It was time to stop being dependent on others.

Something inside of me was showing me that my life was not meant for such abuse. I was much more than the person who would stay there to be bullied. I decided I will no longer leave it to anyone else to put a value on me, not my parents, not my husband, not anybody but myself. I decided that I mattered and was now evaluating myself. It was time to smell coffee Katie a small voice kept saying inside of me.

That is the day I woke up and discovered who I was. It was time to find out what I was made of and the value of my life, to live with respect and love. I was no longer playing the cards I was dealt, I was now going back to the table and demanding a new set of cards. I was not going to go to my parents either, but I was going to stay on the streets until I found out what to do next.

Our culture has treated the girl child like a minority with no value and can be discarded easily. She can be sold like an animal like a goat, treated like an object with no blood or emotions. A lot of us women have not been lucky to live to tell such a story like me because many die in marriages like the ones I had where no one cared to check what was going on.

Although I had no official educational qualifications, I told myself I was going to find my way to survive. I am happy to say that I did find a way, I managed to find shelter, send my children to school, put food on the table, provide medical insurance when they fell sick. I was the first child in my family to build my own house from scratch. But I'm getting ahead of myself.

It was when I looked at the innocent faces of my young children and recognized that I would have to literally man up or girl up as the case may be. I have managed to prove that life without a husband is possible. That's it's possible to accomplish your dream, that's it's possible for you to prove your own self-worth, it's possible to live up to your own potential. I was back to my super power like I had never left.

Let us now get to work with this chapter.

1. Are you a victim of abuse?

2. Do you have someone to turn to?

3. Are you exposing others to physical abuse?

4. How can you begin to get help?

There are many help lines nowadays where you can call anonymously to receive help and if you don't have someone who can intervene in your circle, find some of these at the end of this book.

5 WHEN THE GOING GETS TOUGH

Now beloved, I am all for sex education in schools so follow me as I walk through this experience that I went through. I have found that sex education as we teach it to young people at first there is embarrassment and shyness, then understanding and then curiosity. As sure as we teach science to end up with experiments, well there is experimenting albeit without supervision obviously and you understand that part is obvious.

This prompted me to think perhaps the lessons we teach in biology though somewhat helpful are not complete without including a certain result of the consequences of indulging in sexual experimentation which is that of having children. It is therefore my humble suggestion that a recorder of a baby crying nonstop for several hours a day for a period of the semester to be included in the syllabuses.

I only say this in jest, but this is also an untaught part of sex education and perhaps the toughest and that is, the resulting child that comes from pregnancy. Such an experiment would allow some of our young people to recognize that this is not an experiment they quickly want to indulge in and perhaps save us some heart breaks along the way.

I raised four children as a single parent and they are all just a couple of years apart from each other. This means when they were just babies, they were all ranging from toddler to infant all in the same one bedroom and all crying about at the same time. That is enough to break your soul, especially when you are also by yourself dealing with separation, divorce and then death of a beloved husband who had become estranged from their birth.

Joe, my ex-husband once I had departed, did not live long with his mistress. The party lifestyle was short-lived and perhaps some of those relationships played a part in his quick and tragic demise. I guess the one thing worse than divorce is death of a loved one even if that loved one was now an ex.

It's such a mixture of emotions that I don't know how I ever got through it. Naturally the babies all will look at you with great expectation because to them you are the hero and to yourself you think you are just poor old you. Nothing could have been further from the truth however, as I reminded myself again, looking into my oldest one's eyes, he appeared empathetic as though he somehow understood or perhaps; I was just seeking validation and found it in his eyes.

It was at that moment that I decided that enough was enough. When the going gets tough, that's when the tough gets going and I knew tough was my middle name by now because I had survived it all. It was then when I decided I would find a place in the city and also secure employment. It never occurred to me I lived in a country where employment was scarce.

I had decided that if there were only two jobs going, one of those jobs was going to be mine. I was witnessing the superpower of a girl child whose mind they made up. Nothing can overcome a made-up mind. With nothing more than hope and a prayer I found work with my cousin Noah who was a renowned photographer in those times, and I suppose his name was symbolic to me.

This was me also starting afresh after the flood washed all my matrimonial hopes away. I found my way around the city and networked with various people who also came from my father's town of Bindura who had now moved to the big city Harare.

It was not long after that I found gainful employment in the government as a civil servant.

This was a new chapter in my life alright and I worked extra hard. I was super alert and paid attention to instructions and completed my tasks quickly because I thought that since I was uneducated formally, perhaps; I needed to show up more in my work ethic to overcome that self-perceived deficiency. It was not in vain however, quickly I moved up the ranks because of my work ethic and even though the salary was not a lot of money, I now could afford a roof over my head and a place where all my children could live under one roof for the first time.

When I left Seke I had to send the children to my mother's until I was ready again to have them all together. I witnessed very interesting things happening amongst my colleagues. Many of them were craftswomen with abilities to make what we called doilies and elaborate African dresses that were bright and colourful. These were very elegant and worn by rich women in our time. They were custom made outfits in those days.

As you will recall I had gone to a crafts school so it didn't take me long to catch on to how to make these dresses and soon I had patterns I copied from the original pattern cut outs but since I did not have the right paper I traced the patterns onto newspaper pages and cut them out so that I could reproduce them on my own.

I saved enough money to buy my sewing machine, and soon I was making dresses for sale. By that time I had made a few connections with well to do working women who often bought a few dresses now and then. Initially, I did not price the dresses for sale outside the inner cities yet. It was not until I overheard other colleagues discussing how they often travelled to neighbouring South Africa to sell these garments and how the market over there was very lucrative.

South Africa was going through their liberation war from apartheid so if I was going to do this I was risking my life. I remember thinking well, what's being risky, anyway. You only think something is risky if you do not know how to do it but once you have done it a few times the thing that seemed risky to you is no longer considered risk even by you. I had to latch on to that hope I saw in my baby boy's eyes that day and say I can do this and with that affirmation I crossed that border along with a few girlfriends of mine who had done this journey a few times.

This is where it got really interesting because we soon found ourselves in what appeared to be an old hostel for rental. In that room we were over 15 women and all of us foreigners trying to sell our products to survive. In times like those, you get shocked because you have never been that way before. I listened to the women most of the night as one by one they shared how they were divorcees, abused, neglected and suffered many other traumatic experiences and tortures in their past either from parents, siblings or spouses.

The one thing we definitely all had in common was we were out here to help our families survive. Imagine 15 women in one small room and one toilet and a shower that barely works and yet all walked in a huddle together to make a sale the next morning in a war-torn country during apartheid era. It seems like a movie now but that was my reality.

I want you to think of that picture and ponder it a little. What would make any woman or person risk their life to go through something like that? I can confirm that for me, it was the love of my children, the hope that I could achieve so much more and that this was not the end for me. When I looked at those powerful young women in the room, I could tell as hat they were not quitters either. I could tell the girl child in all of us was displaying her supernatural powers and nothing could stop her.

The market was difficult, but I soon learned that I had a gift of sales technique and honestly when you have travelled for fourteen hours on a chicken bus, slept in a filthy hostel with fifteen other ladies packed together like sardines, you quickly learn that returning home empty-handed is unacceptable for the trouble. I talked to many people who came through the market and displaying a pleasant attitude and maintaining eye contact while selling the merchandise.

I had a gift for remembering names and soon I made friends who lived locally as I would continue to go there on a weekly basis. My routine quickly became working my regular job from 8pm till 5pm then right afterwards, pick up my children from school then sit at my sewing machine after dinner and making some garments, then sleep a few hours and start again the next day.

On Fridays, while some of my colleagues were looking to go to the club as we were in that twenty something age group, I was on a bus for 14 hours to South Africa. Looking back now, I am not sure how I managed it all, but there was no time for stopping until that point in my life it was my best thinking. My baby sister had finished her high school, and she lived with me and it was easier to leave the children with a semi-adult as she was also attending Elsa college, learning to be shorthand secretary.

My youngest son often jokes that your best thinking now is not your best thinking for life, it is only your best thinking until now. He says that in those days we used to carry heavy bags full of clothing called Shangani bags; they were large bags that had two handles and you would put them on top of your head or on your back, however years later, someone came with the idea of suitcases, these were much better, the best for that time or so you would think.

Of course, until someone else put four wheels under the suitcase, making it something you could drag as you went along and that was not the end. Again, it was an advanced idea having smaller suitcases with two wheels so you can sort of walk while dragging them behind you. If you follow this idea now, they even have microchips on your suitcase, and you can programme it on your phone and just have your bags following you. Truly, your best thinking until now is not the limit to your thinking, there is more in that brain of yours.

The point of this example is to show you that the only thing that limits our thinking is our limited thinking. What you are experiencing now may be your best thinking so far based on the ideas you have and the resources you have, but there is much more to you beyond where you are now.

As I grew more aware of what was going on around me I saw that although this was my labour and perhaps my "hustle" as young people call it now, it was not the only one I could have chosen had I had mentorship. This is one of the main reasons I mentor many young people. I want to inspire them to think higher thoughts, to think beyond just finding a partner, getting married and having children.

Of course nothing is wrong with such a desire, but when one has not taken time to know themselves and know what they want in life and are not being forced into arranged marriages as I was, then one must really value their singleness in life.

A girl child must find success in being single, it must become your ambition to be successful and single because a miserable single person will not suddenly make a happy wife in a marriage. When you get married, it is like you are walking into an empty box and what is now in that box is what you and your partner bring into it, if you are not happy and do not bring happiness into the box, marriage will not suddenly cultivate happiness for you.

So, I started off this chapter discussing sex education for young people and here is the reason. If you have learned anything from my story above I hope that you at least learned this one thing, as much as experimenting with sex appears to be a very tempting thing for you as a young girl or woman, once you indulge you may find yourself with children out of wedlock or in a loveless marriage because you and the father may not yet be ready.

Once you bring children into this world, there is no backing out for the girl child. Now the man may walk away and find other options, but as a mother you may find that it is not so easy. While I know I displayed a lot of tenacity in the story, I shared to find a means of survival for my children. Would you not rather raise your thinking and rise above your feelings of love, lusting, or wanting to become prematurely engaged in sexual activities?

This does not mean abstain forever, this means value it for yourself so that it will mean something to you first and then what you value you will not give away easily and you will give it to those who will value you too. While I recognize that this is a noble thought or wish, I also realize that someone reading this book may already have indulged and found themselves with child. Do not lose heart girl child. Pick yourself up off the ground and know that you are not the first or the last, but you are the one that will make it because you have many resources such as this book to help you.

Find value in yourself, define your true worth by writing in a journal who you desire to be. Become specific on how you want to look, how you want to feel, what impact you want to have in life, what your wardrobe will look like, who your spouse will look like, what sort of car you will drive, what sort of house you will have, what sort of life your family will have. Become very clear on who you must become because there is no way of going from here to there if there is no defined plan to get there.

My story was hard to walk through and although I learned a lot, I would not want you or your children going through the same thing. We must transcend the failures of the past and overcome obstacles of the future. One superb way to do this is to align yourself with a mentor who has success in the area that you desire to succeed in, even if you must pay for mentorship rather do that than to pay for expensive wigs.

Find people who can level up your thinking and find good productive friends who are going somewhere in life. Not just people you grew up with, but people who exude direction and purpose in life. While selling clothes in South Africa put food on the table and helped me raise my children, there were other circles that I would later know in life that helped to take me to countries like USA and UK. Guess what those sources were always there and ready for me, but I was not ready for them.

In life, you only receive what you are ready for. What is it that is ready for you yet you are not yet ready for it? Are you ready to grow? Ask yourself the following questions and answer them in the quietness of your own heart.

Let us now get to work with this chapter.

1. Who are you, not what do you do, who are you? Define yourself.

2. Who do you desire to be?

3. What will it take to get there?

4. Who do you know that has made it there and how can they mentor you?

5. What hardships have you faced in life?

6. How can you use lessons from these hardships to overcome in the future?

7. What's stopping you from becoming who you want to become?

8. What step can you take to start becoming free

    from it?

CATHELINE MAHUTO

6 THE SUPER POWER OF BEING SINGLE

Being single is a powerful thing for any individual, be it male or female, but being single takes guts, it takes a decision maker; it takes a visionary and above all that; it takes dedication. A marriage is between two single people and it is hard to have a successful marriage when you have not been successfully single. Being single is a necessary part of any girl child's life and it allows you to grow into the woman you should be, it develops your Superpower. You may wonder why it is a big deal. After all, every desire in us says we need companionship and not only that, but of the opposite sex.

Trust me, I get it and I have been there and as I share this story; I hope you will see how being single can best prepare you for your future, not only for your spouse but for your children too. I know I shared my marriage was an arranged marriage into which I was forced at a very young age but what I have not shared is that I actually had someone whom I desired to be with as a teen and we shall name him Rod to protect the innocent.

He was just a year older than me and we became wonderful friends. It was innocent, what we might call puppy love, but I was actually into Rod and could see myself as his future spouse before the parents revealed a plan to marry me off to another. One day we sat outside in the sand and just talked, and I could tell he had a good head on his shoulders.

We fantasized on what we would want our lives to look like in the future and I remember saying I know I am not ready now but when I am I want to dedicate myself to only one man after I have become somewhat successful as a single person. What I did not know then that I know now is that this was good intuition. It is very challenging to become happily involved in your marriage if you do not feel that you have also gained some level of personal success or accomplishment.

When you are married, you pursue a family vision. Should you find a spouse who has an operating vision well that takes precedence over your own and you can become resentful and create a tug of war in your marriage because you have a vision to accomplish too. If you have a vision and your spouse does not, this is also fertile ground for misunderstandings because you look like one who wants to "wear the pants in this house". If you both have visions and they are different for one another depending on whose carries a more natural leadership in the relationship, you can feel short-changed if you feel that your vision or future vision is now being overlooked. I know you have heard of these situations before and so let's explore being single.

Being successfully single really is about finding your space mentally by deciding who you are and who you want to be in the future. What is your greatest desire, and what will be your greatest accomplishment? What are your joys and pleasures and do you take time to do them free of anyone else's influence? What are your educational goals and how can you achieve them, map it out for yourself?

There are many things you can do, for example, like take hikes by yourself, take yourself to dinner and a movie and buy yourself flowers. Take yourself to a massage parlour and care for your own skin by doing facials and paying for them yourself. You may not have the money to do all the above. If so, do things that are within your means, take walks and watch the sunrise and sunset by yourself, prepare a garden and care for it.

All these things and more build your confidence in your life, you become sure that you can stand on your own two feet before being committed in a relationship where you become dependant on the other person and they rely on you. It is hard to be relied on if you are not yet at the state of mind of being reliable.

When I got married off, I felt a resentment, but I was unsure why and now I know why. My single life was interrupted, and, in my spirit, it was a requirement for my growth. You cannot fool your spirit; it intuitively knows what you need. Had I been married off some five years later, perhaps I would have been ready for that. So that resentment created some kind of attitude I imagine, and that interferes with marriage negatively because we are not on the same frequency.

It takes two whole people to make a whole marriage, not two broken people. When people say I am broken and he can fix me, it puts too much weight on the other person because they are not the Messiah, they cannot fix all your life issues by putting a ring on your finger. Two broken pieces do not make a whole, two whole people make a whole, please always remember this.

Do not seek a spouse because something is broken in your life. Please take time to fix yourself first. I know you have heard the quote "Hurt people hurt people", do not let that be you. If you are successful single, you will also be better for the spouse that you meet, and this may bring you a better-quality spouse as well because like attract like.

I hear you thinking well what if I am already married, and I did not take time to be single first? I have counselled with many young ladies who were in a hurry to be married by their own choice and this may help you. Two single people make a marriage therefore, you must maintain a level of singleness in your marriage. Now before you go off losing your head, I mean define the things that you enjoy yourself by yourself and take time to do those even within your marriage.

One must become intentional to just take time away for a few hours a week, create a white space in your schedule. Put on your favourite music, put the kids away and sit in your basement, take deep breaths, light up some candles and listen to your own thoughts. The point is to be intentional about being yourself and allowing your own self time without the husband or the children. Pay a babysitter for those few hours or have your husband take the kids out the entire day.

I watched a couple break down because of something similar once; they had married very young, just over 21 years of age. They did all the things they did together, went everywhere together which was great but after a while they realized they had different interests from each other, for example, the man wants to watch soccer and the woman wants to go to the mall.

You can imagine that if he misses many games to go to the mall for her, after the fifteenth mall visit there is going to be some kind of resentment right, and the opposite is true, after watching the soccer game and the commentary of the soccer game and the post-game analysis and the future predictions of the game the woman will be red in the face. If you understand that example, then you understand how deep this is and you need time for yourself to become who you must become, even if that is to be a good wife.

The young couple I mentioned eventually separated when at last the woman defined herself as a separate entity from the marriage. She was now what I would term "desiring the comfort of marriage while behaving as a single woman". She became detached from the family because her own desires for what she wanted to do were priority over what they wanted to do. This is not a license to lose your head and go outside of your marriage seeking extra-marital affairs, this is a way to maintain your sanity and be a better spouse for your husband.

When the 'ME' of a relationship becomes greater than the 'WE' of the relationship, that relationship slowly crumbles. This is not what I mean by being successfully single in a marriage. I mean one must be able to set time apart for themselves in order to reflect and work on themselves so that they can become a more potent contributor to the relationship. The focus is on being better for yourself so that you can be better together and not to become a competition to your spouse and find yourself out of a marriage. Again, two broken pieces don't make a union whole, two whole people make a union whole.

When I had married the man whom I considered being my choice, I remembered that at first; we went everywhere together. He was my love who drove a snazzy Opel Viva with pristine leather seats in those days. He was dapper in his hat and suit, leather belt and clean shiny shoes. I was his beautiful new bride with a bright yellow dress, high heels, brown cocoa skin, and beautiful black hair. Sure enough, as we had more babies, I found he excelled in being out and about with his friends than being home with me, and at the time I did not have the tools that I now share.

I ought to have created time for myself too, right there at our home, creating that self-time would have caused much less resentment. Do not confuse being lonely to being alone, even if I was lonely. I needed to find time to be alone and away from my loneliness. It is a mindset that sets you apart. It is when we think the other person is living their best life on our time and our dime, you quickly become a nag coz you think, well, I am just sitting here miserable that the seeds of divorce get planted.

Now, after reading all that I know you are thinking, how will I find time to do all that when my life is so busy. Trust me, it is not a badge of honour for you to be busy; I have done busy, and it does not pay near enough dividends. Every person you will find is busy, and that is the fact of life, so it is not about being busy. The issue is about making time for yourself.

Prioritize yourself within reason and put yourself first in those times and guard them jealously. This is how you build your superpower. Put yourself on your calendar too. Why does everyone else deserve time on your calendar and not yourself? They say love others as you love yourself right, but you cannot truly love others if you cannot love yourself first. By now I am sure you are curious how I made it too as a single mother of four. As my children grew up, they were more independent and so during the month-long summer and winter breaks I would send them to the village so they could spend time on the farm learning to be producers rather than consumers.

During these times, I would maximize on the work that I needed to catch up on. I had uncles and aunties they loved to be with and I would send the group out to them for weekends and also have their children over for some weekends so that we could all find time to do other things with our lives. That was long ago though, but I know that if you sat down and thought about this, you could achieve similar results. I have shared with you many ideas, but I am certain that you can come up with many more ways to find peace within your environment.

Here are some questions you ought to ponder:

1. Have I ever been single in my life?

2. What does being single mean to me?

3. Now that I have a new meaning for singleness, what can I implement to allow myself to grow.

4. What areas of this chapter resonated with me and why?

5. How can I address these areas in my own life?

6. What is the first step I can take towards doing this?

7. When will I start?

7 MY MISTAKES ARE NO WORSE
THAN YOURS

During the 80s there was a song by country singer Dolly Parton that was titled "Just because I am a woman." It was in constant rotation on the radio and often I sang along with Dolly without fully appreciating what she was saying. They say when you are happy you hear the music, when you are sad you hear the lyrics and this much is true. One day on a melancholic day I listened, I heard her say the following words –

I can see that you are disappointed by the way you look at me.

And I'm sorry if I'm not the woman you thought I would be.

Yes, I've made my mistakes,

but listen and understand.

My mistakes are no worse than yours, just because I am a woman.

So, when you look at me, don't feel sorry for me.

You just think of all the hurt you might have caused somebody else.

Just let me tell you this so we both know where we stand.

My mistakes are no worse than yours, just because I am a woman.

Lyrics by Dolly Parton

Presumably Dolly Parton wrote these words around 1973 on her debut album and it does the soul some good to listen to the entire song. However, on that

November day when I listened to it, I came out of that experience with some new arsenal for my Superpower in my heart and mind. I recognized it was time to heal myself from all the pain and misery I had been through so far in my life.

Here I was a single mother of four, late husband, working three jobs, barely sleeping, on the road every weekend, carrying heavy bags and not getting enough rest. After a while it takes a toll on your body. My body announced that we will rest now for a few weeks. I was just burned out from it all and it forced me to take a much-needed rest. I was not feeling well, and I could not tell what exactly was the matter but I certainly knew I was tired so the doctor advised me to rest.

It was in that time I reflected on the words of this song and here is how I was relating to it. Sometimes people that you love hurt you. You do not fully know how to respond to it because you do not expect a husband to cheat; do not expect your parents to force you into a marriage; you do not expect that the person you marry would physically abuse you. You pick yourself up and carry on but then as sure as the sun will shine, those hurts resurface and ask you, are you going to deal with us now? How about now? Ok how about now?

I was ripping and running for so long I didn't have time to deal with the emotional turmoil that had impacted the best of my teenage years and into my twenties. I realized that there were no apologies forthcoming from my ex-husband; he was dead.

There were no apologies from my parents, being convinced they did their best, there were no apologies from the father of my first child. We hardly ever crossed paths.

Since there were no apologies being offered, I decided I would forgive them all without them asking. Now, I know what you are thinking I should have demanded an apology. Hello, how does a dead person apologize? I learned in that moment that forgiveness is not something that I do for others; it is something I do for myself.

I wrote the names of all those whom I had felt had hurt me and the list was long; friends had double crossed me in many dealings with them; I had met people whom I assumed I could get to build relationships with but at that age many would show up married or attached and it rarely took long before phone calls from angry spouses came through on my phone and wedding bands mistakenly fell out of pockets at lunch dates.

One by one I addressed them by name as though they were right in front of me. My script was I would state that I forgive you Mr. or Mrs. So, and So for this and that which you did to me, I forgive you; you are free now and I am free. I release you to your highest good and wish you much success in your life. I did this for several weeks, sometimes multiple times a day, and inevitably it was those who were closest to me that came to my mind many times a day and I had to speak to them again and again in my imagination and forgive them.

I was not oblivious to my own mistakes and I know there were also those who claimed I hurt them by my actions and I offered apologies to those who were still close enough to be communicated with. This process felt good because as I was learning, some of them had forgotten about the matter, some were holding their breath for that apology, some were still angry about the matters. This exercise took a lot of guts because let us be honest asking for apologies is hard, especially when you do not believe that you were wrong.

Then I embarked on a journey that was sparked by the song. I now had to look at my own mistakes where I had wronged myself and say to myself my mistakes are no worse than yours just because I am a woman. Obviously, I was talking to my ex-husband Joe in my imagination but also really talking to myself as a woman, my only actual competition. I recognized I made mistakes and just like others had judged me; I had negatively judged myself, too. It was ok to make those mistakes because that's how I learned to become who I am.

I said to myself while looking into my own eyes in the mirror; I forgive you Katie; really I forgive you. For allowing yourself to be abused by people I forgive you, for allowing others to take advantage of you, I forgive you, for thinking of yourself as anything less than a powerful woman because of your education, I forgive you, for becoming angry at your own family, I forgive you. I did that one for years and continue to do that one to this day.

It is a superpower, and it allows you to stay in harmony with yourself; you know it is so important for you to be on good terms with yourself. Every day you must ask yourself am I on good terms with myself? Being on good terms with yourself is only possible if you are free or unforgiveness, anger, resentment or hurts from the past. That is one of the best places to live your best life from, the place of mercy and forgiveness for yourself first and then for others.

So, the words of the song continued:

So, I know that I'm no angel.

If that's what you thought you had found,

I was just a victim of a man who let me down.

Just let me tell you this, so we both know where we stand.

My mistakes are no worse than yours,

Just because I'm a woman

Lyrics by Dolly Parton

Now it's time for you to put this into practice:

1. What part of this chapter resonates with you the most?

2. Why does that part resonate?

3. Who has hurt you that you are still yet to forgive, write their names down?

4. Who have you hurt and what can you do within reason to offer apologies?

5. What must you forgive yourself for, write it down?

6. What makes it hard for you to forgive?

Now that you have these answers down, begin to create exercises that you can do on a daily basis to forgive those people and yourself. Do this as frequently as morning and night and even though it will be hard at first, eventually it will become easier so that you will wonder how you ever went through life without doing it. Normalize saying to yourself I love you, look deep into your own eyes and say the words I Love You.

8 SURVIVOR SERIES

In the end, however, no one can claim to be perfect. No parent can say they did everything very well for their children. Every parent I have talked with says they have a few things they could have improved when raising their children. The words if I knew then what I know now I would have done better, I often hear them say. I guess the saying is true that when you know better; you do better.

Eventually, I had a room in my heart to find some grace for my parents and how they raised me, although I still had many questions about their judgement of marrying a teenager to a full-grown man. I realized that if they regretted those decisions, they certainly did not let up or show that they felt that way. It was when I was looking at life through the lens of my own children that I found some level of grace to offer my parents.

Since I was not formally educated to the level of my desire in High School, I guess I felt that completing that part of my education was somehow going to fulfill some desire that I had in my life, perhaps just the feeling that I could accomplish that. Siblings can be funny sometimes in life with off the cuff remarks like I succeeded in my GCSE Exams and you did not even get to that level. Those kind of remarks used to hurt me in the beginning, almost as though I am the one who chose not to do it.

So, when my eldest son Sam was now starting his high school, I also enrolled into adult learning High School level. While he was doing homework, I was doing the same homework from the same syllabus so often I went to him for help. I was going to graduate with this GCSE if it is the last thing I do, and perhaps if only to be able to say to the naysayers see, it is not beyond me to accomplish this after all. I was determined to complete this level, and that I did. Then after I realized it is just a piece of paper; it did not validate me.

The challenge, however, came when I was juggling a full-time job, night school, homework, taking kids to school, making garments for sale, travelling to South Africa to sell them on the market. As you can tell, there was hardly any time to do anything else, not even dating and some play time. My children were growing and at one point all of them where in grade school at various levels one in Grade 6, one in Grade 4, the other Grade 2 and last in kindergarten and similar in High School, Form 6, Form 4, Form 2, Form 1 at the same time.

Each child was growing fast and developing their unique interests in sports, dance classes, athletics, acting, piano and much more. Every so often, a letter would request for parents to come and cheer on the children. They had high hopes, but they could tell right away, mommy was not able to make it. No matter how many times I said I was unable to go and support my children in their events, I felt like someone was punching me in the gut each time I said I had another thing to do that was going to put food on the table.

I never got used to it and it was the one thing that kept me up at night mainly because we knew other parents who had both a mom and dad in the house and those parents made it to the events. It is hard to explain that one to a child, either you are showing up or you are not, it is black and white with the children.

When I would look at their faces after coming from these events with trophies and medals, I could tell that there was one thing missing in their experience and that is a present parent. Yet even with that how was I going to do it for all 4 children going through high school at the same time with events on the same day at 4 different schools without a car to get around. I felt that I failed my children in this area so much and that is when I began to find grace for my own parents.

My daddy was a renowned chef and eventually worked in a butchery when jobs became scarce. My mother was a stay at home mother turned farmer. I do not know what they earned, but they sure did not seem like they were banking lots of money. I suppose for such a couple, a dowry is a windfall, it is an added relief for support. Was it justifiable, no? Was it justifiable that I could not make it to my kids' extra-curricular classes, no. So, viewing things through the lens of my children, I realized that I was not doing it all just right and that I could stand to forgive my parents and be ok with how things turned out.

When I reflect on my journey, I was 28 years old when I was divorced by my last husband Joe and left the place with 4 children, zero income, zero support. In that mind frame, it was truly what I term Survivor series, which is a name given to WWF wrestling specials that my children and I used to watch. I had to go into survival mode where you strip out all the distractions and focus on what brings income, health and shelter. This was ok when they were little kids but by the time they grew and graduated high school I was now in my 40s. I had spent the better part of my adulthood catering to my children and my siblings.

That is a mindset that I now had and the dangerous thing about having a mindset is that it is you choosing to set your mind on a particular belief, and no one can really correct you. When you set your mind on something even if it is incorrect, it is your job to reset it when you learn something new but when it has become a way of life, old habits die hard.

It is when my eldest now secured a job and began to help sometimes in the household that I started to find time to relax more and participate in their lives. They had grown so fast before my very eyes. Were these those same little children I carried on my back with tears streaming down my face? They were a hilarious bunch who cared deeply for one another and stood up for each other as well as showed up at each other's schools to support one other.

So, with that said, I realize that everyone needs a little grace and that everyone can improve in their parenting journey and that is wonderful. Yet with all that said, I recognize that unless we are intentional about empowering all our children regardless of gender makes for a greater family in the long run. Empowering the girl child makes for better homes in the future.

It was a song by John Mayer that expressed this so well:

Fathers be good to your daughters

Daughters will love like you do

Girls become lovers who turn into mothers

So, mothers be good to your daughters too...

As a girl child I hope that this book empowers you to see that you have the superpower to be, do, and have what you desire in your life. You have only to follow some of the teachings in this book and you will become wildly successful in your professional and personal life. One day, I had to wake up and realize that I was somebody and I deserved better without the tools that you have right now.

9 CLOSING THOUGHTS

When I look at my journey of my life, I do it with gratitude and I appreciate that I am here to tell my story to tell someone if it is possible. That all that suffering was not for nothing. I have heard that is not how long you live but how much you contribute to the well-being of others that matters most, and I believe it to be true. That is why this book, that is why this project, that is why counseling and serving others is my life's mission.

All these years later I am still amazed that not a lot has changed, the girl child is undermined most of the time even in their own families. The girl child is not empowered or supported to be able to become independent in the future. I realize the status of women is the status of democracy, but this is not acted upon by many people.

As women we do not have equal rights and we do not have empowerment or respect nor protected as women. When I consider my culture, girls are only respected when people want something from them if they happen to be in possession of something of material benefit and afterwards discarded. They do not partake in the family inheritance be it from their parents or where they are married once their spouses pass on; they are stripped of their possession they acquired in their marriage.

When they pass on as well their parents are also finding their way into grabbing those properties, forgetting that they charged dowry in the first place. So, the girl child is up for grabs, she is sold like a commodity; she is not given a choice to make her own decision as per what she wants in her life.

Meanwhile the boy child goes scot-free without even the basic skills of life to prepare for his future. We see marriages crumbling each time because they have no respect for the women in their lives.

I have come a long way to realize and recognize who I am, to have the edge to choose and follow my dreams as I see them now that I am grown up, and I have children of my own. I have learnt from my experiences that children need empowerment, whether it is a girl child or boy child.

I have learnt to respect and love myself and to forgive the painful experiences in life I have gone for counselling so I can help myself understand my life and how to move on without holding a grudge or remorse.

Many parents from different cultures are still practicing this culture of arranging marriages for their children. It is not easy, and it is hard to fall in love under those circumstances. I believe as parents might have practiced and embraced this culture but from my own experience its traumatic to go through this arrangement. I would like to urge parents to empower their girls to become independent and be leaders for the future and be enlightened in life.

Parents should be in front to support their children or women in politics. We see this in the world: women are not free even in their environment be it at home at work women are struggling all over the world.

So, in closing what are the lessons and what can you as a parent do to raise a confident girl child?

1. First, find value in your girl child and treat your children as equals, play no favorites.
2. Offer all your children a chance to grow and explore all opportunities that you as a parent have access to. Do not limit to just the male children but to all your children.
3. Seek to learn from those who have also successfully raised children, join positive parenting training that are available now

everywhere. The biggest room in any parent's life is the room for improvement.

4. Pay attention to your girl child even when married off, be sensitive to her plight and keep communications open.

5. Create intentional times of family discussions where you allow all your family to make contributions as to how to better your own family tree rather than following old traditions that no longer serve anyone.

Girl child, be wise, be renewed in your mind, be the best version of you that you can be. Know that before you are a girlfriend or a wife, you are a person first, you are no less than any male or female. Own it, become yourself, become the superpower of the Girl Child that you are.

Thank You

Catheline Mahuto

Domestic abuse: how to get help - GOV.UK
(www.gov.uk)

ABOUT THE AUTHOR

Catheline Mahuto is a mentor, counselor and advocate for the girl child and uses her story to educate and inspire families around the world on how to better position their female children in a way that can prepare them against the gender biases that they will be sure to face in their lives. She is a mother of four and grandmother of 11 and great grandmother of 3. She uses her wisdom , knowledge and understanding to help young families through counseling and mentoring primarily in the United Kingdom.

My Photo Gallery

My many faces

My son Samson

My beautiful grandkids

CATHELINE MAHUTO

Made in the USA
Monee, IL
01 November 2021